WORLD THROUGH MY GLASSES

A COLLECTION OF 100 NARRATIVE STYLE POEMS HIGHLIGHTING DIFFERENT THEMES AND EXPERIENCES

ANNETTE MENEZES

Made with ♥ on the Notion Press Platform
www.notionpress.com

Contents

Contents

Contents

Contents

Contents

Preface

After a 21 day, 21 poems challenge that got me winning the 21st century Emily Dickinson award I got inspired to continue writing. From an initial target set to 50 poems, I reached out further to complete a set of 100 poems. Phew!

The poems are visually descriptive, using figurative language, like an imagery to create a lyrical emotion.

Acknowledgements

I am truly thankful to God almighty for having given me the confidence and will power to finish and create an inspiring poetry book with utmost dedication and passion for writing.

I am thankful to my son Nishad for having edited and helped me publish each of these poems, and for always motivating me 'Never to give up'.

I am grateful to NOTION PRESS for giving me the backup support needed with regards to publishing.

1. Beat The Odds

Life's a journey
With many a dream
It takes many a milestone,
Sometimes even scale a mountain
To achieve and succeed

There's many a set back
Confusing thoughts that contemplate;
The good, the bad, the ugly
The goal to accomplish -
With time in every passing phase

There are obstacles, you may encounter
With stiff competition that, keep you stressed out;
Sometimes it's a roller coaster ride,
Keeping you engulfed to sway with the tide
Stay afloat although you may falter -
For its just a win that matters,
And it will come by sometime or the other

The future may seem distant,
The past has gone by

Wake up to the present,
Let go off your ego and pride
Try, try and you will succeed -
It's all in your positive thinking,
In putting your best foot forward,
To taste the essence of life, that's sweet

Sometimes you are in a race to conquer
And may, miss out on key aspects, that define
To make or break the shackles, that underlie
At times, in turmoil and you wonder why -
When the best times roll before you,
In the blink of an eye

So wait and watch out,
For the opportunities, that strike
At times they come, once in a while
As the saying goes 'Make hay while the sun shines'
Make the best of whats in store -
There's always a chance, so dont let it go

Hold on to your aspirations
Like the wind to a sail!
Cautious, but fearless, to the stroms you face
Plan to navigate and steer,
With a definite target in mind
Unwavering to fall prey to strife -

ANNETTE MENEZES

Beat the odds and 'Let it show '.

2. Count Your Blessings

The miracle of life is your first blessing,
One that's truly God's intervention
When we wake up to a beautiful day,
It's manifested with happiness
It's blessing is one of natures bounty

We fail to see, the expanse of our surrounding,
As we are so engrossed with day to day living;
The urban streets, the vendors call,
Disturb the silence of peace and tranquility
But they are a blessing equally

Head to the neighbouring mountains and fields,
Breathe in the pure air that's unpolluted -
Make time to relax and unwind
Feel the exuberance, as its , a blessing indeed
Your God given talents of art, music and creativity
Don't waste it ,but get it nurtured
And with it seek happiness,
That speaks volumes of your blessings in return

Your health is your wealth,

So eat right, with self control
Plan a routine and diet if you must-
Never let go off your thoughts
As good health is a blessing to claim,
Don't waste it, but nurture it
And with it find fitness in return

Be prayerful with gratitude and acclaim!
As there are so many homeless
And struggle day in and day out
The poverty around us, is most times ignored
So be thankful, for all that we have
As it's a blessing to behold

Our family, our friends, our kith and kin
Those who help us in our need
A listening ear, when we are in trouble and pain
Spoilt for choice with luxury
With countless blessings in plenty

We have the wisdom, the knowledge to learn;
The ability to know, what's good for us
We have the choice, to gadgets that make life easier
So seek these blessings and you will find,
That God has given us plenty -
Be grateful at all times
Make use of things sensibly,

Learning to save wisely
As each of these, is a big blessing to life.

• 6 •

3. Follow Your Dream

There are dreams, that make and break you
And instantly awaken you,
If you have dreams to fly,
Don't let it lie
There's something in your subconscious;
That comes to light

It might be a distant dream or vision
Or a past unfurled to reason
But, give it some thought
And your dream, would take you on
To some lessons untaught

It could take you to a future,
Sometimes unexplained
And you wonder, why you got there
When fears invade
And make you question, if it will ever fall in place

Sometimes you picture, a sweet dream
Which draws you to think positive
So you go after it to persevere,

Bringing forward, that much wanted desire

The key to your dreams is within you,
You grasp on to it or let it go
At times, the dream persists
That you need to win over it
And hold it close, for results to show

It could be dodging back and forth,
Maybe frozen like ice
Leaving you blank faced,
Or perturbed in turmoil
Like a cracker that just burst forth!
Of what was in sight

At times, you want it to linger on
As your memory, goes for a toss
When your dream got vanished into thin air
Leaving you forlorn and lost

Sometimes it feels real,
Within your control
At times, the night blinds you
And sleep overtakes in time,
To let it lay dormant within you

So follow your dreams;

Reach out and hold on tight
You never know, how far they lead you
As luck favours the brave
Believe in yourself and dream big,
To achieve and make these dreams
And see a breakthrough.

4. Soul Stirring

When the plants, flutter in the breeze
And the cool wind blows on your face
When the early morning dewdrops, you see on the leaves
Wakes you up from a daze;
It's a soul stirring gaze

When you see, a stirring performance
Or an act, that's par excellence
When you hear, a beautiful medley
And in turn, it gives a thrilling experience
That is soul stirring, to the mind

At times a wildlife adventure moves you,
It could be just a monkey chatter
Or seeing a bird that twitters
And maybe a butterfly that flutters;
It's soul stirring to your senses

When you win a game Or do something conducive,
You are deeply stirred and moved
By the praises you receive
When a peacock opens its feathers;

ANNETTE MENEZES

It's soul stirring indeed

When nature's bounty, is seen in all it's colour
The hue of the sky and the rainbow yonder
The pitter patter, sound of raindrops
To spot a shooting star
It's soul stirring, to watch and wonder

When you see a creative display,
Or an artist at work
It moves you to admire
The many brush strokes it takes,
To complete a picture
Giving a soul stirring experience to capture

When you do something out of the ordinary,
Climb the highest mountain or do bungee jumping
You get the exuberant feeling of achievement
To see a lion roar or a tall giraffe in motion
Leaves you mesmerized at its stature
That's indeed a soul stirring moment

When you see a trapeze artist swing from a rope,
Or a boggling magic trick, that keeps you engrossed and in awe
When the spider builds it's web
And the weaver bird it's nest
It's a soul stirring moment that tugs at your heart strings.

5. Mother's Role

Let's begin with the babe in the womb
The mother nurtures her offspring,
To be safe and secure
Her nine months of gestation time,
Is a time she waits patiently
To take care until she has a safe delivery

She takes all the necessary precautions,
To remain healthy and strong
As she feels, a sense of protection
While her body changes proportion, by the baby that grows
When she feels the baby kick within her womb
To get a thrill of joy, to its living

Her hand gently caresses, the baby within
As she waits, in anticipation for its birth
While her cravings to some foods
Are let loose, although a healthy dig matters
Taking the months that lie ahead;
To picture, motherly grace and eloquence

When the day of birth finally arrives

When she holds the baby in arms
The labour of pain, that comes with childbirth is forgotten
As she sees before her the embodiment of love

Her protective instincts bears an example of lasting bond;
As the tiny little bundle
of joy
Sleeps to cuddle close;
She is woken up to sleepless nights
Of feeding and cleaning, also pacifying a howling baby at times

She has no time to whine,
As the baby keeps her fully occupied
The work is done clock wise, without complaining
As her motherly instincts, are inbuilt and no surprise
For to love unconditionally and sacrifice her needs,
Are instinctive to her nature.

6. Mum Knows Best

She is up at dawn,
With no time for a yawn
And no time to laze around
Her mind is full of thoughts,
Of what to dish out

For there's ironing and cleaning,
And kids crying and wailing
She puts out, an armour of patience and understanding
She has no time to fuss, or do make up
Yet, the little time she finds
She is multi tasking, day in and day out

The time in between, she reads the days news
Watching TV, awaiting the online delivery
Planning the menu for the day,
Tends to washing and clearing the clutter away
It's time to open the internet,
For her childs classwork is underway

She waves goodbye to her better half
Whispers a prayer, with a deep sigh!

To protect and keep the family safe,
As her mind wanders awaiting
The maid, who does not turn up
And the day goes by in a jiffy;
The good times, the bad days roll on
From going behind, the crawling baby and the yelling child
She fumbles and runs, to protect the falling child
To kiss the bruised wound
To hug and caress and even sing a lullaby;
Then to feed and sterilize the bottles
To making a cup of coffee,
To refresh and unwind

The child by then is asleep,
The day goes by, without a whimper
For there is no time, to ponder
It's a daily routine of total surrender;
For the hand that rocks the cradle!
To being a MOM is no wonder.

7. Out of the Woods

Out in the woods, there's no one but me
As I am lost, among the wooded trees
With shadow and darkness around,
That makes me fear the unseen

Why in loneliness, did I venture
Lost in thoughts, I wonder;
Was I longing for an adventure
Or I kept wandering, without realising danger
That I was alone in a situation,
Amongst the maze surrounded by darkness

As I carry on, towards the direction of light
Confused but determined to find
For I know not, where am I ?
As I barely see the sky
The route I take is unclear,
And doubts of clarity appear

Could I encounter someone-
Who helps me along the way
Or get tied up with, a feeling of helplessness

To have gone astray, my mind gets boggled
As I do not find anyone near
Showing a clear cut path and insight,
To bring me out to finding daylight

It matters most the direction I take,
Find a firm ground and footing
To venture out, from dreaded trails
That leaves me in a exhaustive state
I need to be calm and relaxed,
Focussed to move on and take courage,
To get going from the wooded nightmare
From being lost in despair
To finding the right road to success
And be victorious in the end.

8. Pave the Way

Pave the way, clear all roadblocks
Be sensitive to your needs
Take all the required support,
For there's much to understand
When life's mysteries come along the way

What you sow you reap;
Plant the seeds of goodwill
In whatever you seek,
There's much happiness to gain
While you get blessed in heaps,
Keeping you focused to leap

The road may seem bumpy,
With many problems on the path
Weed out the bad and take control
They are stepping stones, from failure to success
From bearing barriers that you foresee

Sometimes the road is less travelled;
Leads you to venture
Into new and unseen terrain,

To get hooked to something approachable
And explore possibilities
To take you closer to your desires

Don't follow, herd mentality
And imitate what others do
Take a new direction
At times it works well for you
You be the director,
And pave the way for your future

You are the best judge;
And it's all within you to advance
Get hold of the best
Take your chances, play your cards well
It's your mind that matters, which paves the way
And everything good follows thereafter.

9. Be the One

Be the change, you want to see
A helping hand to others in need
Be the one to sport a smile,
When all around you seems gloomy
Be the one to share your thoughts
Ignite ideas, when all seems lost

Be the one who instils belief;
Giving confidence to others
Maybe a pat on the back,
To make the day special
Be the mentor, be the guide
To enlighten many a life

Be the one to give good advice,
Caring and giving in nature
Be the one to solve a problem,
Never to lose with hope and time
Be the glue that binds together,
When troubles you encounter

Be the one that instills faith,

When everything falls apart
Be the bond that gives strength when
all is lost
Be like the candle that glows
And brightens up the day

Be the one who makes life better,
Caring and giving by nature
Be the one who lends a hand,
When things seem to crumble
Be the prop who makes the hard times easier
And the good times sweeter

Be the one to show concern
In many ways to love
Be the one, to connect and show closeness at heart
Be the one to hug and embrace,
For in giving you receive much happiness.

10. On a Good Note

Start the day on a good note,
Meditate first with gratitude
Watch the sun beams seep in through the window
And the early morning calm, of surrounding nature
That relaxes your body, mind and soul

Feel the crispness of the air,
And the fragrance of the flowers bloom;
The eagle that soars high above
And the white clouds that pass by,
Create a picturesque display, in the sky

The birds that perch on the treetops to call
The squirrel's that run around
The pigeon that coos, at its partner
Only in silence you hear
Smell the aroma, which wafts in the air
Of brewing hot coffee
To start the day, with a good mood

Listen to soothing music,
And let your mind wander

Maybe an yoga posture, with eyes closed
And folded hands, in prayer meditating,
Maintain a work routine to time
With a written list to remind

Follow a systematic schedule,
Probably a time table
Doing what's essential,
Keeping yourself occupied
Take a start to doing things, to keep you happy
And your passions to explore
Begin the day on a happy note.

11. An Artists Den

The palette is a riot of colours,
The brushes dipped in oil
The folded canvas is opened,
Which awaits the artists eye

The easel stands tall ,with the clip board in place
While the artists mind is sombre,
And the outlines visioned to focus
In what picture to unveil

The imagination runs wild, to explore nature's landscape,
Or a still life of a fruit bowl placed
The hand begins to take it lightly
And with each brush stroke, moved to define

The mind is engrossed, as there's silence around
Each shade flashes and blends,
To the form and shape it takes,
Of the background, that depicts to show
The artists spectrum to create

The picture unfolds, in all it's splendour,

To the keen eye it's lost in wonder
The artist at a glance, is never satisfied
In an intense moment, of losing patience
To do touchups, splashed around with haste

But perfection to detail is being creative;
Changes made to be innovative!
Every angle is crucial,
For the artists work to be special
Until the moment it signifies,
That it can hold, a pride of place
In the viewers heart and mind.

12. Memories

The key to happiness, lies in having memories;
Remembering good times, brings the past back to life
Old photographs each tell a story,
To remember times, spent happily

Unlike the digital pictures of today,
That sometimes do get deleted
It's the age old, black and white albums,
That make you grin, smile and laugh
That are a treasure you cannot deny

Your childhood memories are your best ones,
As the joys of innocence, is portrayed
They bring back memories, to reminiscence
With loving people, whom you grew up with

The naughty and toothless mischievous look,
The fashions back then
The frilly frocks and stilettos,
And bell bottomed pants
The thick glossy, coconut oiled long hair pleated,
That sports a now old fashioned look

The grizzly curly mass, of thick moustache
That gave men, a serious stern face

The top hats and tailored coats,
The polished boots and broad ties,
The beautiful, crochet and applique works
That gave a royal regal style

The ceramic and pure steel cutlery,
The easy rocking chair,
The high doors and ceilings, with tile roofs
The horse drawn carriages, cannot be found
As they turned, antique and rare

The stain glass and etched windows,
With the wooden, venetian blinds
The wrought iron ,designed gates and stairways
Speak of an era, that's unique to find

The Kennels for dogs to sleep,
And the wooden rope tied swings, that swayed really high
The weather cock, that showed wind direction
Showed memories, of the years that whizzed by

The stamp collectors albums and greeting cards,
And letters received by post
The old crystal chandeliers, that hung high above

The wooden lofts and stone benches,
Explain a bygone era that's gone fast

The autograph books and ink pens,
And old tin trunks to store
The bell jar covered candy floss, entice your taste buds
Are memories that are steadfast

The milk in glass bottles,
The lemonade sold outdoors,
The garage sales with discounts,
Brought out a curiosity in you
For these were lasting memories, that changed to modernity.

13. Resonate

Feel the early morning sun, resonate the warmth
Feel the rhythm of your walk, as you stride along
See the reflection of light, that resonates bright
See the emotional response, while you speak your mind

Hear the voice, that resonates within you
Hear the silent echoes, of what you believe is true
Keep the emotions that resonates, from the heart
Keep your exoerience that made you feel good in the past

Strike a chord that resonates harmony
Strike a strong message to promote unity
Relate to a signal, that is clear in thought
Relate to a passage, that resonates a knowledge path

Take a positive feeling, that resonates deeply
Take an opinion ,that's accepted widely
Make your life significant, that resonates a good story
Make it powerful enough, to value it completely.

14. Simple Joys of Childhood

When the circus was in town
And the top tent was seen high above;
It brought immense joy,
As I waited for the clowns to arrive

Going to the fair and riding on a merry go round,
Choosing the horse or the elephant to sit on
It brought giggles and laughter,
As your head spinned after

Hearing the candy man down on the street,
We rushed to find a coin to give
As we chose, the bright pink and yellow colour candy
It brought a thrill, to see the colour streak on your tongue and
lips there after

When we learnt, to make paper boats
And sailed it through a puddle, of rain water
It brought happiness, as it swirled and toppled instantly

Bringing immence joy thereafter

When we flew newspaper kites
And it went high up in the sky,
It brought a smile on our faces
To see it flutter in the breeze,
High above the trees

When we made a pyramid, from a pack of cards
And laid each one carefully, so it does not fall
It brought a smile, of achievement
When it remained sturdy, for long

When we bought and chewed gum,
And blew the biggest bubbles to compete,
Until the bubble burst, flat on our face
Which brought a smirky grin on face

When we took the cycle uphill
And came down the slopes, in gay abandon
Balancing through, ups and downs
It brought on, a top of the world feeling

When we took a ride on a toy train,
That chugged along slowly, over a small bridge
And then went through, a small dark tunnel
It brought a shout and scream of excitement,

Although the ride ended abruptly

When the stray puppy, was brought home
And we secretly kept feeding and wanting it as a pet
The joy of it, jumping around
Kept the desire to adopt,
For the simple joys of children's love for animals, was brought out
to care.

15. Celebrate Success

When you are down and out
And you try your best to move on,
You celebrate success

When you feel hurt and disowned
And you take courage to get up,
You celebrate success

When you go through hard times
And you use patience to continue,
You celebrate success

When you are in pain and dejected
And you use your energy to renew,
You celebrate success

When you have the doubts
And you question, to get your thoughts right,
You celebrate success

When you know what you see is wrong
And you go all out, to correct and make a difference,

You celebrate success

When you feel cheated and let down
And you use wisdom, to fight for your rights,
You celebrate success

When you fail at times
But never let failure discourage you,
You celebrate success

When your work load increases
And you stay calm although it tires you,
You celebrate success

When your past hurts you
And you change to better a future,
You celebrate success.

16. Nature's Freebies

You are the sun that, shines brightly and warms my day
You are my vitamin D, I don't have to pay
Most often you get too hot and then sweat me out;
On a cold winter's day, you hide behind the clouds
I cannot complain too much,
For you are nature's freebie after all

You are the star that brightens, the dark night
Although it's just a flicker, you light up the sky
You make me gaze at you in wonder
Since you are so far away,
I wait to sight you, when you appear and sparkle
For you are nature's freebie that twinkles

You are the wind, when the day turns warm
Sometimes you are still and not blowing around
I wait for you on a hot summer's day,
Knowing I need the breeze, to cool me down
For you are nature's freebie that I could count on

You are the moon that takes the spotligh,t
Sometimes you play hide and seek

And i wonder, where you disappear at night
But when you reappear round and full
Or just come out as crescent;
I am so overjoyed at viewing you,
For you are nature's freebie that is fabulous to watch

You are the sea with so much water
You are so inviting, that I love to dip my feet
And walk on sandy shores;
As a child I built castles and played with buckets and spade
I loved watching the boats and ships sail, on the far away ocean
I was thrilled to see, the waves go high and collect shells
For you are nature's freebie ,that gets me happy and content

You are the stream that gurgles down your path
You come rushing with force,
To be a magnificent waterfall
I cannot lose sight of you,
As you are breathtaking to view
You keep me so mesmerised and in awe,
For you are nature's freebie, that's beauty without doubt

You are the mountain that's higher than a hill,
You are the showstopper, as you are tall in stature
When I make the climb to the top
You keep me engaged ,never to give up
And once, I achieve this feat

I watch to stare at the far horizon
For you are nature's freebie, that captured my attention

You are the plants, the trees and the grass
You are of different sizes, growing wild in the deep
With pastures that are green
And stubby bushes with rocks scattered between;
You are the landscape that meets my eye;
That keeps me engrossed to stare, at the river flowing near by
For you are nature's freebie that provides life

You are the air that we breathe,
You remain fresh and unpolluted
Without you we cannot survive,
For you are the elixir of life
As in a steep hill ,it's difficult to climb, when your temperature
drops
For you are nature's freebie, that keeps me alive and kicking.

17. Sheltered

As humans we are born to be sheltered
From the womb, where the babe is nurtured
When the child cries out loud
The loving hand reaches
To soothe, comfort and cradle

Out in the pouring rain,
The stranger who does you a favour
Offers you a lift and shares your umbrella
By that gesture of kindness,
There's an outpouring of love and thoughtfulness

When stressed out and fallen apart,
Crestfallen with no one around
That someone who gives a listening ear
And gives support easing out your fears,
Gives you hope and dries your tears

When the mind is not at peace,
You are restless and dejected
But that arm around your shoulders,
Keeps you calm, from your depressed state

You find the genuine act and feel sheltered

When you are sick, frail and weak
You are unable to find relief
And there's that affectionate voice that you hear,
That nurses you back on your feet
You experience being cared for and indeed sheltered.

18. Be Fierce

Fighting for your rights,
Is being fierce to survive
To face the critics,
Got to be passionate to your needs
Only then you overcome hurdles,
Fiercely lighten your burdens

Fear is your worst enemy,
That stops you from moving ahead
Take courage and be strong,
As life has its ups and downs
But it's in you to hold on,
Fiercely facing the storms head on

The inhibitions of not knowing,
Might keep your thoughts misplaced
You may misjudge to contemplate,
Treading On the rough trail
May encounter a rough start,
Fiercely using tactics is a must

Being timid is a sign of weakness,

Leaving you left out in the end
And taken advantage there after,
So grab hold of the best, that's seen
And the best will come back, in return
Fiercely showing brevity, to carry on.

19. Reality

Knowing the reality of what's to come
Change in circumstances and not be rigid to set norms
As a matter of fact, reality cannot be defied and strikes hard
To change and accept is a must

When in denial of what's new,
Take for granted to be stubborn, as a mule
As reality cannot be taken easily, for it's there to stay
Unless you turn against it, keeping it at bay

To be realistic to your present needs
Keep it simple, follow the leads
The past is always there, to haunt you
Take the future, in your stride
As to be in sync while it dawns,
When it dawns on reality

When the situation is bad,
And the feelings not right
When things seem unreal,
You are too far away to be heard
It's the reality that unfolds,

To be bad or even unwise.

20. Teach Them Young

As parents we are first teachers,
Your child is your focus
They imitate you as you are the role model
Teach them right and they follow likewise

The child's behavior comes from your source,
With the upbringing you provide
The knowledge you instil,
Remains as foundation to their lives

As they learn from observing,
It's the right guidance that matters
Both at home and at school
Add a blend of love with discipline combined

Teach them to be good human beings,
Be an inspiration using patience as a key to child's success
Never undermine and let them down,
Give praise when required

Do not pamper, do not spoil
Use words of kindness and advice

Give a listening ear, never ignore
For you are, whom they turn to
While facing the problems, they incur.

• 45 •

21. Reflections

Resting under the shade of trees,
Swinging from a branch to thrill
Gazing at the skies above,
While the sun rays seep in
Walking carefree, reflecting the past

The events of time, eventually break away,
From the impressions of adult life
When the conflict between the old memories,
Transition to reflect on the new

While I am engrossed in my thoughts,
There's a vision clear, with a reminder
To find myself a shield to protect
And view the future, with what is at stake

When your spirit guides the message you receive,
Your undaunted and fixed to your needs
Taking each day, as it goes by
Reflecting on what's best to your future

When my mind is at rest,

Like the fresh blooms of spring
Gather the good fruits of labour
And reflect to overcome, the hurdles,
In finding success.

22. Liberated

When Hands are bound by chain,s
When oppressed with hardships
And you are brave enough to fight,
To untie the limits of bondage
You are liberated

When you struggle to find freedom,
To find knowledge and bliss,
That elevates your true being
To get wisdom in return,
You are liberated

When our country, is free from tyranny
And our land is free of hostility
It seeks independence to our identity
And find the true sense ,of living peacefully
You are liberated

When there is social transformation,
To have gender equality
And gain equal status
And we are transformed yo find unity,

You are liberated.

23. Pages of Life

My life is like a book,
The pages are open to me
As I flip through, I find many a memory
I remember mostly the good, as the bad I tear off quietly

They are reminders of somethings I have achieved,
As they are there, to showcase my good deeds
Each of the lines boldly written,
Cause I faced them, through thick and thin of seasons

My diary gets full with time
It's in my heart, soul and mind
Sometimes discoloured with misuse,
Like the pages of a rough book
At times tattered badly,
When I'm stressed or met with tragedy

I want each page to have substance,
To bring value to my writing
Enhance and get better each day,
Without cat's whiskers and blotches

Beautifully lettered, with each passing day

To fill up the pages of life that's happy,
I enhance each line with hope and faith
That the result of my writing,
Brings out the best book,
That gets to be a perfect read.

24. Bridges

The bridge I cross, should always be strpng,
Whether it's narrow or broad
Build great friendships with a bond,
That's lasting over years

The bridge should give me a path that's pretty,
Without hurdles and strife
Take me safe to where I'm headed,
With a view to see what lie's ahead
And a better future in sight

The bridge over waters is scenic,
Should take me across smoothly
With people who care and love me,
Like the river that flows, with calm waters
Much like the boats, that sail ashore

The bridge of peace is unity
The pillars held with respect, to all religions
Cemented with tolerance and patience,
Building bridges of a loving nation.

25. Highs and Lows

My morning coffee gives me a high,
When I wake up subdued
It puts me on my feet, to begin my day, on a happy note
Warming up my senses and spirits to soar,
It's the brew that energises me
From the feeling of being low

When I am down and stressed,
Famished by hunger pangs
With, a hard days work load
It's just a snack, that puts me on track
That rejuvenates my gastric juices,
Putting me on a high
From being low key

The highs and lows in life find place
Itis all in adjustment, to taking the right perspective
That you find solace in accepting
Finding answers when feeling low,
To bringing success and getting high with victory

When you search high and low, to find a firm footing

From the grassroots, to a stage of prosperity
To being elated and highly spirited
From the feeling of being down and rejected,
It's all in you to make it happen

There are friends, who walk in and out of life,
When you are highly successful
You are surrounded by them
But when down and low, you come to know a true friend
For the ones who care and support
Are like true gems ,in the midst of storms
Calm you down, from your lows.

26. Door to Happiness

The door of my heart is always ajar,
To be loved and accepted
It remains loving, to find that someone
When lonesome and lost

The door opens wide to anyone dear,
Who pours out affection
For the feeling is mutual,
When you are in gloom and face rejection

The door sometimes shuts,
When disdain with cruelty
You know you need a shoulder to cry on;
When you are down and forlorn

The door at times, closes with a loud bang
When it's outraged with anger
You need that calm to overcome
Then meet with serenity to move on

The door sometimes remains locked,
When emotionally cut up

It takes time for your mood to liven up
And to find happiness back on.

27. The Face in the Mirror

The face in the mirror does not lie,
It speaks the truth and does not hide
It reflects the years that you cry,
It also sees you smile

It portrays your emotions,
Draws your attention
While you grown and grin,
It mimics your true profile

While you see yourself, with that sad look
With cheekbones withdrawn,
To a poker face sometimes
To watch and seek correction

When in a good mood,
It views happiness
Making you fall in love with yourself,
While it mirrors a blissful look, of calmness

I am who I am,
With each a mystical smile
That draws you to notice
The flaws, the imperfections, you see with time

My stature works for aligning
And gives the perfect pose
To bring out that best look
Of beauty and confidence

At times the mask is on,
Hiding my identity
Yet it's ready to show me
Without explaining, who I really am and my personality

Oh mirror give me the clear image,
To know my true self
That I cannot change, the face I see
And to know that it reveals honestly.

28. Looking Inspired

When I look at my childhood,
I know I was inspired
By my parents who were my first tutors;
They guided and taught me values,
That made me strong to overcome
And face life boldly, without fears

When I look back, I see the many friends
Who inspired me over time
And they still are around me,
Even if years have flown by
Although some are far and abroad,
They do keep in touch and am happy to find company

When I look back at my school and college days,
The ones I met inspired me
There are distinct memories,
That lie clear in my mind
Of the beautiful times spent together,
Besides studies, fun, frolic and laughter

When I look back and see that my children have grown;

They are my inspiration
As to what I taught them when small
I say with pride and all,
That they are a blessing to reward
Thankful to God, for guiding me along.

29. Babes in the Woods

The barking deer, barks hearing, the sound of the forest jeep
It's eyes show fear as it protects;
It's doe in the green
It does not run instead, gives a warning stare
Unlike the other deer, that dart away

The elephant calf, it's mother and the herd
Moving playfully, always nudged
Not to stray, but move along slowly
Close to it's peers, within its boundary

The lion cubs are sheltered,
As they prance around within proximity
The lioness hunts down its prey
And the little cubs get to it ,,before the pride
To sink its teeth to feast on

The tigress that looks fearsome,
Must look meek before it's cubs
Protecting its young one from predators
As they stride, into the deep terrain

And if spotted, to see a majestic walk

The crocodile with its hatchling,
Stays without moving like a stone
It's mouth open wide, while it's prey is unaware
As it stealthily, catches it in a jiffy
The frog between it's jaws

The Wolf remains within its territory,
Devours on elf, rabbit and mouse
Its pups litter in the dens
With the male alpha, the leader of the pack,
Look fearsome with gritted teeth to claw

The bear looks huge and grizzly,
And weighs heavily
As they pound on with their sows and cubs,
while scared of blaring noises,
Of sirens and horns

The rhinos remain solitary,
Unlike the female bulls and calves
Which are more sociable and mingle freely,
With their male counterparts
In their own vicinity

The hippopotamus with its calves,

Love to eat food and grass
It can swim to be a water horse
And as pygmy hippos, consume leaves and roots,
From the thick forest undergrowth

The journey of a giraffe with its herd,
Towers slowly around at a great height
It stays standing in short cycles,
Sometimes lying down
Eating shrubs and vines

The cheetah with its spots,
Leaps fast when on the prowl.
But is slender and weak
Vulnerable to threats ,
From big cats and hyenas that hound

The hyenas look aggressive,
When frustrated they laugh out loud
With high pitched giggling sounds,
The babies born underground
In dug up holes by mother hyena,
To protect from predators around

These are wild species,
Their existence is mandatory
The need to protect and keep them safe,

To roam free in the jungles
Without glaring eyes of the hunters
And protect them from extinction;
To keep our ecosystems functional.

30. Awaken the Inner Child

The child in me is spritely,
Sometimes waiting to explore
While the hippocampas lies to be patted,
Like the sleeping baby that wakes up from slumber
Needs to be fed when awakened,
Before it brawls in hunger

The child in me is curious,
Sometimes waiting to know,
Of what's happening around
At times stubborn in nature,
Like the Buffalo that lies still ,without moving
Even while, it rains and pours
To remain unmoved, without a care in the world

The inner child in me is bored,
Sometimes wanting to ignore
Although there is many a lesson to learn,
Needs motivation like a bird, that spreads it's wings
To take it's first flight, out bold

Without knowing if it could,
And once up in the air
Remains steady like it's fold

The inner child in me is scared,
Sometimes fears the worst
It takes time to overcome,
And encouraged to try,
Like a tight rope walker in a circus
Takes his walk boldly, to be cheered by the crowd

The inner child in me gets emotional,
Sometimes cries out loud
It takes time to calm the feelings,
In getting back to a good mood
Slowly mustering the right moves,
Like the baby. which falls taking it's first steps,
Gets up again, with a guiding hand
That supports and cares

The inner child in me is smiling,
Sometimes thrilled and content
It wants to share happiness and make life worth living
Capturing all the good times,
Much like a photographer, that focuses well in getting an
awesome picture
That gets everyone's attention and at times a candid picture.

31. Chances

Life gives you many chances,
To live and let live
It's the changes it takes,
From the choices you make
To dream, explore and take the steps
One by one in confidence

Life has many things to offer,
Many paths, that lead you to choose
At times leaves you confused,
By the circumstances, that are hidden
But you need to find the right way
And direction, that does not leave you astray

Life has its destiny, that you cannot foresee
It's up to you to figure out , the best ways
That take you on and lead you to a smooth journey;
To manoeuvre through a maze
That's deceptive and can change

Life is difficult to conquer
And at times loses track

When in dilemma of what is good;
So set your goals and targets
And shed your inhibitions,
To relax, be cheerful and explore.

32. While in Silence I Think

While in silence, I think hard
The thoughts are baffling
When the silence is broken,
To take the good path
As silence helped me get answers

I sit in silence when hurt
The mind is confused and curt
In the quietness I feel the urge,
To let my feelings out and about
As silence helped me find solace

While at the crossroads I sigh!
In a dilemma, of which way to take
When in silence, I contemplate
Whether it leads me rightly;
As silence helped me choose wisely

In silence I feel calm,
The peace of tranquillity

As I sit alone like a yogi,
Close my eyes and surrender my mind
As silence helped me meditate and move on

While in silence I am alone,
I encounter distractions that disturb
The very recesses of my senses,
Blocked by dead ends that detour
As silence helped me overcome them all along.

33. Unleash Your Potential

Success begins with your potential,
To get to know your weakness and faults
The strength that comes, from your passions
While sometimes, you deter and fall
You wake up to determination,
Getting the best results

Practice makes perfect they say
And hard work pays
But the outcome of victory,
Remains in being steadfast to commitment
Mindful of competition and awareness

Making learning, enjoyable and interactive
Putting in efforts and quality time
To listening and observing, to latching to views that define
To solving problems that undermine;
The seeds of wisdom lie within you
To surge ahead and envision a better tomorrow

When the tide turns never let go
It's an opportunity, as the many elements of life begin
With second chances to improve
The learning curve scales up,
To unleash your potential
So never give up.

34. Legacy

Each of us have a history
The good we do turns to be a legacy
The impact you create,
Leaves a lasting impression, which will be passed to generations

While you dream for a legacy of knowledge
You impart the good, you desire from the world
To better your future prospects
Of a legacy that leaves;
A lasting impact to your present

Making a difference in life,
By your generosity and calm
The love shown, to create
Handed down to progeny
Plays an important role, in your life and family

The chapters of your life you depict
You are your life's author;
The choices you make,
Is the legacy you inherit
By your own deeds and actions,

To a fine legacy in the end.

35. Flavour to Savour

The good things in life, are bitter sweet
For they end up, as health benefits
The sour lemon with bits of ginger
With a blend of honey,
Starts the day that's refreshing for sure

The salad that's colourful to look,
Have the best nutrients to suit
The carrots are a binder
The purple cabbage gives a blend;
To a simple vegan diet to end

The oats and porridge at breakfast,
Adds a healthy dig
To a muesli that has almond bits
For a cereal that stomach fills
Your good breakfast needs

Hot water with a dash of turmeric
A drizzle of honey to sweeten
Will warm your throat
And is also a good way,

To get your stomach lining, in order

Like the clove, that relieves a tooth ache
And coriander water, when strained and kept overnight
Is a good eye cleanser, when filtered
Are remedies, that also add spice as well as flavour

The bay and basel leaves
Have a lot of taste, when added to curries
The peppery rasam, had on a cold day
Is light to make digestion easier
That in turn are flavours to savour.

36. Uncertainity

We are powerless, when there is uncertainty around
The thirst for knowledge is a common cause
It outlines and plays a larger role,
That fulfils mission and goal

When the nation is at war
And the fate of innocents, is at stake
When the grappling soldiers, fight it out
And the wounded, stare at their fate
The world stands still with, a crisis

There are emotional flare ups
And their cries unheard
Shaken up, to violence and aggression
That gives doubt to freedom
Drowned in fear and sorrow

Life has its uncertainties,
It's with courage, that you put yourself forward
To make the best of the way, things turn out
And wade through the swirling stormy waters
To keep yourself afloat.

37. I Believe

I believe and hope for good things
Like an innocent child, who does not know, the intricacies of life
But when put to testflight it out,
To try to fly high;
Like an eagle that soars

I believe and admire beautiful things
Like going window shopping
I try to possess and strive to get them,
Come what may, own to buy and fulfil
My dreams and desires galore

I believe, I deserve what I earn
When I work hard, to succeed
There's no one to stop me
For I hope to make it happen,
To reach the top ,as I am confident enough

I believe, I can reach for the stars
When i trust my capabilities
For my mind knows the trials ,I have faced
And choose to get better-

To taste success in my future.

• 79 •

38. Go Green

My heart though pictured red
Melts to see a beautiful green scenic patch
The parks, the footpaths, lined with trees
Is the lung space, that every nature lover dreams

The well manicured green lawn
Are a carpet ,you could lie on
The beautiful canopy or flowering tree
Is something for your eyes to feast
And a perfect place for birds to nest

A green area or a topiary to add;
Adds beauty and is a nature's paradise
The butterflies that flutter around
And the bird that twitters, brings a melody
To a biodiversity of space

Protect our trees, from being felled
They are our oxygen supply
And we co -exist side by side
For our economy system, to survive
Plant more trees and let our land revive.

39. Tiger Snarls

Tiger Tiger burning bright!
Glowing orange against the dim forest light
The bold black stripes ,that determine
The majestic glory of the wild

Save me from the hunters eye
The gun shots that fire the bullets sigh!
As I run to nudge my cubs,
To protect and run for cover

But alas!
They are too tiny, like kittens
Playful and attract attention
With their beady eyes and low volume snarls
While the predator watches the prey, to hunt down

The cubs are always in danger
And most do not live beyond a year
The tigress on the prowl;
Gives out a great intense cry, to protect

His majesty is never safe

From being killed and gunned down
As the taxidermist eyes, it's fur and skin
And the big teeth, as good luck charms

Protect me from the cruel monsters, that defy
Follow the government rules that preserve Wildlife
From being extinct, as the numbers are decreasing
Keep me protected, from the hunters gun

Hear my snarls, hear my roars
Do not let me fall prey
Let me dwell safely in the forests
For I am meant to be wild
And the forest is where I lay

Watch me not, when I am caged
But left free, to stroll in my territory;
For that's where I belong
Not to be hung as a trophy.

40. Listening Ear

The head has not heard, if the heart has not listened-
The quote says you give a ear, only to the one you love
The listening echoes within you,
To put your heart and mind
That manifests your hearing too

A broken soul shuts out hearing
It ceases to listen and to viewing
The one that offers to give a listening ear,
It is truly a big comfort
So never let it go

Most often we fail to understand
A smile, a good word, an honest statement
That could change our life around;
If only we could hear and know it's potential
To believe in the goodness, it shows

When we choose to see and find the good in others
You feel the good within you
So be the one, to give a lending ear
To see yourself listening too

And all in all, works wonders for you.

41. Roots

Roots are a foundation laid,
To a better tomorrow you make
To the strength you derive for your future,
Depends on being well rooted
To ground reality to that of your past

The town were you grew up is distinctive,
Because it brings nostalgia to the fore
Your roots spread ou,t from your school days
Become stronger, to absorb, the good in store

You may grow up in different cities
And meet different people with time
But the roots stay put, at where you left them
To encounter and go back to renew energy, once in a while

You get emotionally attached, even if far away
To be cared, loved and feel the attention
To find familiar roots ,that cling together
Like a mothers love and devotion of a father

To see familiar surroundings,

The roads and bylanes new look
A wee bit different, but never lost and forgotten
To get back , to finding roots at intervals

The memories are always steadfast
And very dear, to be strengthened with obsession
Like a long lost relationship;
Deep rooted and always stand as beacons.

42. Follow Your Heart

When in dilemma, of where to head
Follow your heart, it tells you the best
The road to success is never easy
Most often, it's in contemplation, of what's to be

When you lose sight of the present,
And wallow in pain
It's a bittersweet journey,
You learn from its mistakes
And follow your heart, to cope with it

At times, you are broken and fragile
And need time to recoup
But move ahead and find a safe harbour;
Follow your heart to seek refuge

When you focus on your past,
You lose sight of the present
But nevertheless, follow your heart
For it always, is there as a solution

When you walk on paths, that have hurdles

But you have the uncanny ability, to get past it
Do not judge or be judged
Follow your heart and your intuition.

• 88 •

43. Those Magic Moments

There are many stars that twinkle bright,
But it's the one star that stands out
From the many you see in sight
In the far horizon

Everyday seems special,
If you make magical moments happen
Happiness is not measured by what we have
But enjoy the little things that bring joy

Life in itself, is a moment
There are many creatures on the ocean shore
But just s starfish, lying dead in isolation;
Catches your eye, to a moment you cannot ignore

The flowering tree that blossoms
A snow capped mountain
Creates a beautiful picture,
That's magical to see and endure

The chocolate dessert, the hot cocoa drink
The fireplace, that warms you
On a cold winter's night
The quilt you cuddle into, are magic moments that warm you

When you find freedom, in a quiet moment
All alone in your own space
Away from the nitty gritties of worries
To create a magic moment, of peace and solace

Lost in a crowd you look for a familiar face -
when all of a sudden, you get that affectionate hug
From the one who loves
It's a magic moment to seize indeed

When you look down at a newborn infant
Or see a bride and groom, arm in arm
When a child, learns to walk and speaks his first word
These are magic moments for a parent to feel elated.

44. Chosen Genre

An artist, a painter, an author a novelist;
Has a chosen genre to create
Like a song writer who writes lyrics
And a musician, finds a rhythm to it

A designer sketches on paper
A new and unique style
While the model, walks the ramp and flaunts it
That steals the attention of the fashionista

The variations and intricate patterns,
Attract an art lover to the canvas
While the beauty lies in the eyes of the beholder
It's aesthetic looks, bring out an emotion

To be a celebrated artist or writer,
And receive accolades takes effort
While passions are set ablaze
To find imagination ,that runs deep rooted

Your works acquire a dynamic character,
That has refined over time

But you are never satisfied and find reasoning;
To portray and let your feelings show

You are constantly trying to set a bar
In finding a niche, to recognition
And getting to success, by choosing
Whats best suited to your passion.

45. Motivated

When the time to fare well,
Lies in being motivated
At times,. it's difficult, to get past failure
But if motivated, to put your mind to it
In all possibility, it can be achieved for sure

Motivation is the key in your workplace,
The fuel to your desire
Stay solely with your belief,
And find that inspiration
To stay focussed, to your needs

The internal force, comes from dedication
And in turn, imparts direction
To strive and get motivated
And with a lot of effort, get going
By putting your best foot forward, to find the making

When you aim higher
And motivate yourself to reach for the goal
You get closer to winning

And find success in return

To remain motivated,
Never lose interest
Develop a timeline, to complete your tasks
And condition your mind, to take charge.

46. Break Toxicity

Have you ever felt powerless,
And cannot raise your opinion
Are you at a loss for words
And treated from speaking, out in open
Well the power lies within you, is lost to gender discrimination
To voice out,as we are subject to ridicule

Male dominion is seen even today,
Bossed around by chauvinistic men
Who think, they are in control ,of the woman
Like predators who glance
As if she were a commodity,
Meant for display or caged up
Not allowed the freedom, to keep her identity

When egos clash and the man presumes he is mighty
This narrow thinking attitude,
Handed down by society
To think that men have the upperhand
And can use a woman to be a slave
To serving his selfish needs,

To be dolled up for sex and beauty

Well the power within the woman.
Lies entirely in her hand
To fight for equal rights,
To remain on par with men
But this can only happen ,if the views of society change
For a status that respects her, as equal an important

Break the chains of disparity
Bring down superiority
Maintain a balance of equality.
To create a sense of well-being
By facing the stronghold of male bastion
To give importance, to withstand adversities ,with resilience.

47. Throw Out of the Window

Throw out of the window abuses,
Do not target it to use
Throw out negativity,
Ascertain a positive attitude

Throw out of the window,
Clutter that disturbs
Throw out heartache,
Let in a fresh breath instead

Throw out of the window
Your pride, which prevents you, from going ahead
Throw out ego,
Be simple and watch your patience grow

Throw out of the window, unwanted gossip
That disturbs your peace of mind
Throw out garbage talks,
That blocks you from thinking ahead

Throw out of the window,
Stress that keeps you depressed
Throw out evil,
Find a way to see good instead.

48. Finding Beauty

There's beauty in the butterfly, that flutters around
The colours of the flowers, it sits on
As it draws itself to finding nectar;
It's nature's beauty, that we see is spectacular

There's beauty in the trees that bloom
Canopies like a colourful umbrella
The carpet of flowers, that greet you
It's nature's beauty, in all it's spendour

There's beauty in the fields,, that meets your eyes
The sunflower, that turn to the sun
The ripe sugarcane and corn, that sway in the breeze
It's nature's beauty, that captures your sight

There's beauty in the mountains that's scenic
The expanse, of the landscape that's gratifying
To feel the cool air or find the warm sunshine above
It's nature's beauty, that is glorious to watch

There's beauty in seeing a waterfall
Cascading down from a height

To get the spray of water, on your face,
Is a delight
It's nature's beauty, that gets you awestruck

There's beauty in the gurgling stream
That flows gently, as it winds down it's way
To get your feet dipped in its icy waters
It's nature's beauty, that gives you the thrill to enjoy

There's beauty in a well maintained garden,
When you find the white pebbles
A topiary and a sparkling fountain
It's nature's beauty ,that gives you happiness and joy

There's beauty that needs to be found
And you make the effort, to find
At times the joy of little things, like a rainbow
It's nature's beauty, that keeps you engrossed to glance and see.

49. Roses

Every beautiful rose, has its distinctive name
They all look pretty to see
But this beauty, has made you reason
That this one rose, has a season
As it blooms and brings joy,
Also withers and wilts before your eyes

But it's perfume lingers on
The scent as strong, it engulfs you
By its varied colours
There's always a rose you admire,
Among the many that you see
They are a riot of shades, that meets your eye

Every rose has its thorns,
Pierce you deep, if you are not careful
But these roses, need to be cared for
Pruned, cut and sprayed, from pests
For the plant to get it's nourishment
Manured and watered to get
The perfect roses to admire!

It's perfume stays even, when the petals fall
Made into a potpourri, as a decor placed in bowl
It adds charm and is pretty to look
Placed in a vase, to remain fresh
Made into a bouquet to celebrate, an occasion
A pleasure to accept always.

50. Growing Up

When the kid in arms,
Finds its strength to take its first step
And the parent watched to see it's growth
While it's weaned, and nurtured
It's growing up

When the child in school
Finds friends and companions
And learns to listen ,when taught
To sit attentively, to care and share
It's growing up

When the child in its teens
Finds wisdom and knows to get along
And to speak and relate well in company
It's growing up

When the youth feels confident
Finds maturity in thinking
And learns responsibility, to take on a challenge
It's growing up

When the adult knows, where he stands
Finds a firm footing, in the work front
And handles pressure with ease
It's growing up

When the senior citizen knows how to cope
Finds patience and handles stress well
And gains respect, in the community
It's growing up

When in old age you are not a burden
Find happiness and manage,
Handle well to financially live
It's growing up.

51. Healing

Healing comes with time
When in sorrow and grief,
To overcome losses and move on
Takes a whole lot if inner strength,
And inner courage to move on

The feelings and emotions,
Do not go away easily
The memories stay in,
It takes some time to recover
As eyes swell with tears, when you remember

Healing is a process, that takes its path
Loved ones always, remain steadfast
There's no one, who could fill the void
The recovery is slow paced to find
But as years pass, healing keeps you going on-

It's hard to bear, when you lose someone
And the thoughts keep rolling back
To the good times you've had;
But healing comes when you remember,

To keep the memories, alive in your heart.

52. Just Remember

To relive the past, is to remember
While those thoughts flow
Memories of yester years, are meant to stay
Find memories return in many ways;
Just remember!

It may be your happy childhood
And the carefree life you led
Dreams that creep in sometimes,
With happiness, combined to share
Just remember!

To await a celebration, that's yet to come by
That which alerts your brain, once in a while
Or it's a flash, of a happy moment
That signals a long lost love
Just remember!

The music of the past, triggers joy
The band, the songs, the dances that are heartwarming to recall
The fashions, the costumes, that remind you of your youth
While you have, the don't care attitude

Just remember!

The parties that carried on till dawn
While you danced, until morning
Your family and friends that cared,
Were your support and anchor
Just remember!

Your school, college and alumni
That made you, your best
The society, the surrounding, the environment you grew up
You recall with gratitude as a blessing
Just remember!

53. Acceptance

When you learn to accept failure,
That there are ways to success
These difficulties of knowing, not to give up
But make do with the situation
Is acceptance indeed!

When you learn, to let go off problems
And try to solve them, with humility
When you have the right mindset,
To overcome and adjust
Is acceptance indeed!

When you learn to take decisions
And use wisdom, to sort things out
Respond rightly to circumstances
By solving issues diligently
Is acceptance indeed !

When you learn not to be aggressive
And use kind words and speak calmly
You bring about, an understanding
To get answers in a mature way

Is acceptance indeed!

When you learn valuable lessons
Follow them with integrity
You gain respect with control of emotions
And behave a well balanced person
Is acceptance indeed!

When you learn to overcome stress
You use patience as the key
You unlock a great deal of happiness
To take decisions in a composed way
Is acceptance indeed!

When you learn to accept your wrong
And take things in the right spirit
You get to correct yourself
And take it in your stride
Is acceptance indeed!

54. Parenthood

The charm of being parents,
Gets better, when children learn to adjust
They observe, your ways and actions
And imitate you to follow instructions
The job of parenthood is successful

The children turn, to your good guidance
If you show by example
Show them the way, through affection
They take your advice and support
Making parenthood easier to handle

Make them your friends and teach discipline
By giving an ear to their problems
It does not matter at whatever age,
Your love and guiding hand
Makes parenthood all the more easier to earn respect

The transition of a child, to being a grown up
Does not end at any particular age
It's having someone to look upto
As parenthood is a process

And it does not have, a stop or fixed time.

55. To Be Loved

As a kid I ran happily,
I found love all around me
The kiss from my mother, when I had a fall
Nursed me back to smile thereafter

When I cried out loud,
I got the attention I needed
The hug and reassurance of my father
Who affectionately carried me on his shoulder

As a child I found love amongst family,
They became the centre of my universe
I found the caring, around me
And the warmth, I felt, I did not need company

In my teens, I found friends who loved,
So I held on to, good friendships
The few who gelled with me
I felt happy being around them

When in my youth, I tarried around people
Went to groups, that made me feel right

I learnt to choose companions, who put me at ease
For I knew, where I was loved, happy and pleased

Then the union of two people, finding each other
Came marriage on the cards
It happened like magic all at once
The foundation to our meeting, was based on love

To add to growing up, sharing with caring
The base of love was solid to find out;
That living together as one
The essence of happiness ,was to be loved

And to be older with age
The turn towards everything, was love
When circle of extended families and friends grew larger;
The focus became truly to love and be loved.

56. True Companion

I found you alone, among the many I knew
You were the face, I constantly saw
You were the one, I could trust
For I put my feelings at rest, within your heart

You were constantly, in my presence
I missed you, when you were absent
Your closeness and strong bond, I felt
When you always put, my my mind to rest

You knew me well, even when I was silent
Your voice echoed within me, at times when I was lonely
I could feel your love, which was silent
When you spoke to me, even when distant

You held me close and I felt safe beside you
You gave me the support, when I needed you
You understood me, even when I faltered
You were my true companion, I revered.

57. Made My Day

The day is perfect to stroll
The weather is nippy and cold
Yet the peace and calmness,
And the relaxed time I get
Makes my day, perfect in every way

When I've had a hard day at work
And I get the time to lay down
And sit in silence for a while,
With only my thoughts in my space,
Makes my day complete in every way

When I am around people,, who make me happy
And feel welcome in their company
And they are there when I need them the most
I feel brighter in their presence
That makes the day gratifying in every way

When I've achieved, something I desired
And I find contentment in my work
And see the joys I gain in return,
Find blessings coming my way;

Makes my day fulfilling in every way.

58. Humanity

Humanity is a race against time,
To live well and be tolerant
And build a better tomorrow,
Is our responsibility
Humanity teaches wisdom

Humanity is vast and we are a speck on this earth;
It's to love and love has no religion
To believe in the good of people,
As love has no boundaries
Humanity teaches love

Humanity is to be considerate to needs of others
To show kindness in giving
As giving makes us in sync as humans
Humanity is a reason to believe

Treat each other with dignity and respect
To be humane and mindful of each other
As we cannot live, as an island any longer
Humanity finds unity in caring

Humanity stays with reality,
You find the touch that cares
You be the conscience to choose,
Weed out negativity and restore hope
Humanity finds a need to serve

Humanity finds happiness,
To choose joy in giving
It teaches many lessons
And to be human to living
Humanity taught us to share.

59. Antique Chair

The empty chair on the terrace,
Once stood in the sun
The varnish all tarnished,
It's paint faded out
The wood had a dried up look,
That had gone old with use
Could see the moss around the edges
The nails held its legs jutting out;
That gave an antique rustic look

It brought memories of it's owner,
As it lay in the corner
The grainy look, took a beating
Unpolished, waiting to be refurbished
And treated well to be placed,
Under the roof free, from further damage

Restored to good looks as a reminder;
Of the man who sat
When thoughts came, rushing back
And sentiments to cling onto, it's antiquity stayed
Although, the urge to give it away, was brushed aside

ANNETTE MENEZES

Keeping the emotional attachment alive.

60. Loneliness

As I sat lost, in my own thoughts
I felt alone, with no one beside me
And loneliness crept silently
It took advantage and never left my side
As I stayed cocooned, on my own
With just four walls, that waited for me to head out

I felt it's fears and shed some tears;
There was no one around, to console me
I had nobody, to share my emotions
As I cried alone, with no one to listen
When time stood still and my thoughts evaded me

I looked around for company;
Found no one to support me
The silence around kept pining,
For someone who loved and cared
And spent some time, to keep me company
To let my loneliness, disappear quickly

I heard my own breathing
And the wind whistling and the rustle of the leaves

I looked out, of the window
And found, just the breeze blow
Loneliness, kept crawling in
As there was nobody , in near proximity

So I tried to sing a tune
And take a book to read
Time flew by quickly,
When I wrote something creative
It opened up, my mind and brought joy
And loneliness vanished soon

As I kept myself occupied
And chalked out future plans
My ideas kept me busy,
To form my own strategies
And time flew by in a jiffy,
To find myself, I needed no company.

61. Entrepreneur

I found the freedom, while I was on my own
My ideas beckoned me, to start my own company
I did not fear the failures, or know about success
It's always a question mark, of what to expect

I knew I had the passion and drive within me
To latch on to my conviction, to head on boldly
I never knew of the outcome,
Nor did I think of uncertainty

All I felt was a bold desire,
Put myself forward to hire
I took the risks, to find myself to employ
With the boldness to surge ahead, in time

The business had it's ups and downs
It was not a bed of roses, yet I dreamt on
I worked hard, for i did invest
Reaching my heart out, to be passionate

My aims were high with a target
So I put my best foot forward

Sometimes going the extra mile,
To accomplish and achieve what I desired most

I burnt the midnight oil
Sometimes, losing sleep
Come what may I had to find,
To taste sweet success in time

To climb the ladder, is a slow process
You need to balance and manage, when problems arise
To manuevre and motivate yourself;
In order to reach your goals and target

I took each step cautiously
Keeping in tune, with market needs
Never losing focus and hope
Waiting for the right moment;
To surge ahead patiently.

62. Preserve Our Planet

Have you heard,, the twitter of the birds
Nesting in the tree that lives.
To save them from being axed down
Is to preserve plant life,
As it's our oxygen supply

Have you ever viewed, the landscapes
From the mountain high above
Have you breathed pure air, which is a fresh breath around
Did you find the way, to climb to the top
Preserve the environment for a better future

Have you explored the forests
And see the power of greenery unfold
Have you noticed and felt, the need to protect
To preserve the trees, from getting felled

Have you seen the rivers, that run down it's path
It's nature's elixir and eco system uncovered;
Have you seen how much it offers,
In preserving and saving water

Have you seen the ocean
And the dolphins and whales swim
Have you looked at sea creatures, that keep you amazed
To preserve its beauty, is our duty

Have you done enough to help
And to show you really care
Have you treated mother earth, with respect
To preserve its gifts and not let it go extinct.

63. Visionary

I sleep and lie to visions,
I cannot deny
To envision comfort,
While I stay in my surrounding
Driftly the night passes
With dreams left alone;
With distractions around to stare

My thoughts swayed by
But I still cared
I could not find time,
To make it meaningful
As the day passed by quickly
And I left things hurriedly;
With a mind uncertain to stress

I looked to move forward;
My head held high
To join forces, to make it happen
And see myself, going ahead
When ideas flowed before me
To vision and focus

To view strongly, without regret

And then the day dawned;
In all its glory
Anchored and steady with integrity,
While I took each step slowly
To finding a firm footing
That gave me the confidence,
As a true visionary.

64. Rekindle Hope

When all is lost and wartone
And innocent fell to bullets sound
Hiding for cover, to save themselves
From the wrath, of destruction and harm
To rekindle hope in life alone

Within the hearts, of the soldier at war
Is love and affection of the family
To fight and get back to normalcy
While they hide, in their barracks, lest they be searched
To rekindle hope, for country alone

To get going, bearing the chilly weather and scrotching sun
To do Or die be the slogan, and not be a quitter
To survival instincts of bravery haunt
With no thought of what, the future holds
To rekindle hope to survive instead

The guns ablaze, the bombs placed
The army camps, bustling with the wounded
The last breath, of the dying heard
With no time, for tears and to bid adieu

To rekindle hope to live for tomorrow

The tents pitched, to be together as a unit
With uniforms ,that camouflage
The food in packets distributed,
With just enough to satisfy hunger
There is no thinking of tomorrow to mourn;
To rekindle hope, for victory alone.

65. Lessons Learnt

Everyday is a lesson learnt,
Some are bitter, with an example
A lesson with a motto;
Teaches you to get better,
Wired to the norms

Each lesson brings a story,
With a moral and a theme
The value it represents,
Fuels you to read
Conveying a message to seize

Every lesson learnt,
You find mistakes you've made
Faltered, to correct self
To learn from others
The need to be inspired

Everyday I better myself,
To think differently
I poise myself to seasons

When nature teaches and gives a reason to act accordingly

Every action and behaviour learnt,
Builds a character
The teacher and the taught, both learnt
Success, through sheer hard work.

66. Got The Inspiration

Inspiration is the key, to motivation
You cannot set sail, unless inspired to do so
I got inspired to write
And took my pen, in hand
Made my ideas flow

I found inspiration in little things
A picturesque view, at the seashore
I took out my sharpened pencil,
I got inspired to sketch and draw

And took some paint to colour,
Made my imagination flow
I discovered my talents lately,
Never knew, I had it in me

To sketch caricatures and portraits
I got inspired by artists
And took to learning from there,
Made my boredom go

I found gardening as a hobby

And tried my hand at it
To plant seeds and saplings,
I got inspired to grow more
And the joy, I got, when seeing flowers
Made my happiness show

I found music, that makes me happy
And tried out singing
To join and sing in choirs
I got inspired, by their voices
And with it came the thrill,
Made me feel elated and happy

I found that dancing, keeps me fit
And tried different steps
To keep with my rhythm and fitness
I got inspired by dancers movement
And with it, I joined a performance
Made me feel lighter once more

I found that, I got attracted to artefacts
And tried to be creative
To recreate out of waste,
Got my artistic talents flow
And with it, I got engrossed to, doing handmade things
That made my joy complete.

67. Hue and Colours of Life

Hues of life, filled with bringing celebration
By the warmth, of cheerful chatter
And happy communication
The hues lighten the mood, with music
As you dance to happy tunes after

Hues of life are vibrant,
By a flowerful array of flowers
To add beauty, in the garden
That greet you when you walk
As you enjoy it's fragrance!

Hues of life are joyful,
If you find yourself smile
To keep away stress and depression,
By making yourself worthwhile
As you relax and enjoy

Hues of life are bright
When you focus, on getting your health better

Eat wisely and exercise,
By having self control
As you feel light, adding years to life.

68. The Palace Within

Attracted to grandeur and splendour of ornamental aesthetic
jewels that glitter
My eyes reach out to admire,
The magnificence, of a palace yonder
Added by the beautiful sculpture
It's palatial wonder, of architecture

But do we see nature
And it's divine creation
It's natural springs and waterfalls;
The starry brightly lit sky
Added by glistening beaming rays, of the sun
The daylight seeping in, at dawn
The dewdrops on the green lawn
It's a palatial spectrum, to admire

Do we see the hand of God stretched out in glory
When we see, a miracle happen
That someone reached out ,to help you
And you get something by chance;
That hand that supported you
From falling down and protected

Was it a stranger or layman
That helped you, when you were forlorn
It's the potential feeling, of contentment
Of God's grace and favour from above

The palace within, is beautiful
When it has all the warmth, other than wealth
The happiness and added laughter,
That gladdens up your heart
The palace within , is spectacular
When we have a broad smile
It lightens your mood
To find a spirit, that's light hearted
Filled with exuberance and charm.

69. Desires of the Heart

At first, I was sad and lonely
With nothing to reach out
I desired, to be happy and drive away my fears
I needed love

At first, I had the eagerness
To do something extraordinary
I desired to get better
And worked hard
I needed inspiration

At first I had the inclination,
To get to live better
I took a stand, to improve ways
And find myself, a target to achieve
I needed motivation

At first I had a vision,
To view things differently
I gave it my best, to succeed
And I nearly got there

I needed support

At first, I had an ambition
To move ahead with a goal
I aspired to reach there quickly,
Keeping myself afloat
I needed patience.

70. Find That Niche

Lost in a world, full of things to offer
I looked around to see, where I fit in
With the inclination to have, a firm footing
To find the niche, to stay in

To walk around, awestruck while exploring
To gaze at many things ,I don't need
I just need to see, the right place
To find the niche I desire, to be in

Lost in a world full of people
I get attracted, to things I admire
With walking aimlessly, without conviction
To find the niche, to happiness I desire

To achieve in getting, what's in sight
To find room, for the one thing in mind
With staying focussed to reach;
To find the niche to succeed.

71. Reach For The Stars

Looking up at the sky, I saw a zillion stars
The shooting star, suddenly emerged and dazzled
Brightening the night sky, flickering in the dark

They looked so close, yet so far to reach out
It's like a dream, to latch on
To my starry mind, to focus and shed light
But it isn't as easy, as it looks
As stars beam on, as they twinkle

To look up, you see them shine
To find myself focussed, but they vanish before my eyes
It's like the lazy eyes, that sleep without working
To find myself neglecting, when time flies by

As my mind feels boggled
Given up before, I even try
And so I seek again in desperation, to find it
To remain constant, just like the stars
To reach for them, to being consistent
To find myself aiming high.

72. In Your Space

To be having thoughts undisturbed;
Was left alone to ponder
The freedom to do my own,
In my own little space alone

Unfettered by distractions
With my own creations
Found many ideas, to getting ahead
In my own little space alone

Needed the time to think
And my imagination flowed
Separated from, the rest of the world
In my own space alone

The real world, whizzed by
The bumble bee, buzzed around
My mind was focussed
In my own little space alone

The feeling of being separated
Gave me, my me time

All alone cocooned, like a spider in the web
In my own little space alone

Was in rapt attention
With no one to put restrictions
Deeply conscious, of finding myself
In my own little space alone.

73. From Dawn to Dusk

The sun embraces, the morning to a new dawn
As it rises in the horizon
It brightens and seeps in, through the trees
Waking up early birds .from their slumber

It's radiance and glow is welcoming
As it creates a spectrum, that's a splendour to watch
The rays of light, seep in the twilight
Wiping out darkness early on time

The view of the bright new day, is spectacular
Only when you wake up, to see it's bright light show
Every dawn looks for a new day
As of today, you know not of it's tomorrow

Every dawn is a new beginning
It has its possibilities
Until, the day turns to dusk and the sky darkens
Making the best of everything, for answers to show

Dawn and dusk, go hand in hand
They both rise and set in time

It gives a message, of reasoning
As the light of dawn, fades to dusk
If you do not keep to its timing

Every dawn is a shining example, of light to darkness
It's gods creation and gift to mankind;
To see the light and also embrace it's darkness
To be the ray of hope, of today's dawn
Bringing on a new tomorrow, from its dusky morn.

74. Glimpses of the Future

I know not what the future holds,
The future I cannot control
The glimpses, I see today
Are fragments, of my past displayed

They lay in bits and pieces, like a jigsaw puzzle
Strewn all over, to be identified
From the glaring mistakes I made
To correct and get going, to carry on

The future I view, comes with success
Shedding some light, to what is today
The contribution to the future, lies in a solid past
That has a foundation like rock to stay

To glance and look back, is not in view
The glimpses, just whizzed by
The treasures I got, from working hard
To capture some, the others I let go.

75. Triumph of Adventure

The thrill of adventure, knocked at my door
To go off roading, with my daughter in her Nano
So we decided, to just go without prior planning
To take the drive to Chikmagalur awaiting

The beauty of the hills and surrounding,
Just beckoned to explore
Untarred roads and mud tracks
Which led to open fields and terrains.

We had to head back, to the main road
In time before it got dark
So she took to driving fast
To see myself, enjoying this sudden adrenaline rush

The wheels screeched, the car sped
As she drove through, a herd of buffaloes and cattle ahead
The fear of them biting and attacking
Left us with no option, but to slow down

The adventure became more exciting;,
As the car swerved with every turn

No google maps were helping
To find our way to return

And so we stopped, to ask a shepherd
The way to get back, to something familiar
Meanwhile the evening, turned gloomy
And darkness engulfed the area

And then the fear of reaching, came about
To a safer place to stop over
Happy to have found a town, with wifi around
To take a small lane, that google pointed out

Alas the ride, on the narrow stretch was a disaster
And the car, got stuck in the muck
To make us fear, the unknown, with no one around
As the car was dangling, held by strong tree roots
The only option, was to get out

As darkness fell, we saw a group, of people approach
And sensed danger, to be surrounded by strangers
But by the grace of God, they were good samaritans
And helped rescue us and the car, from falling down
A twelve foot dug up canal

On either side it looked precarious, through just a mobile
torchlight

While our worst fears of the car tumbling, came trickling in
One of the men, took hold of the situation
And the others gave a hand lifting, while one accelerated

The final heave! Was a success
As the car moved slowly and jerked ahead
To reach safely, through the dangerous stretch
A triumph of adventure, to finally reach your destination ahead.

76. Do Not Waste Talent

I owe this poem to my son
As he always, encouraged me to create
As writing became my passion
He enrolled me, to a poetic challenge

To complete this task, without hesitation
To winning the Emily Dickinson award
I found the initial glitch, to finish
And my head was filled, with phrases and rhymes
To jotting down instantly at times
And once completed, I strived hard
To get past, the initial 21 poem number

So here I am in my seventy sixth
To get to reaching, the target of 100
From sheer determination, of aiming high
To achieve and not waste, 'God given talent'

Why the initial 21 poems I asked?
And then knew that, after you cross, the initial number
It becomes a habit, never to give up
So here's my effort and success achieved;

Which may inspire you, never to quit.

77. Search for the Good

Make the most of everything,
Remain true to yourself
It's in finding out, what's good
And remaining strong and focussed

Find the good, amidst the bad
Find the friendships, that mean well
To keep you cheered and faring well
To remain in good company, as well

Seek for solace, find the peace
With prayers, that keep you at ease
Find God's mercy and love
In all that matters overall

Be thankful, live with gratitude
To find happiness around
There are lot of ways, you can steer clear
For worries to disappear

Be on guard, be secure
Search for goodwill and love that endures

To find confidence and trust,
To build relationships that last.

78. Visualize a Tomorrow

While I visualised a tomorrow,
My imagination ran wild
To find a clean world,
Free from smoke, garbage, pollution
Without worries and a clear breath to find

I formed a mental image,
To dream of a better future
Not just for us but for humanity
And pictured, a better tomorrow
That has no discrimination and enmity

I looked to see our roads without potholes;
Free of drugs and addiction
Where children remain safe
And find the confidence, to grow
In an environment, that's secure

I dream of a United world
Where peace and common brotherhood dwell;
Where the child has an upbringing

With freedom, that makes him better overall

I view tomorrow, as a day that has hope
With blessings in plenty
To visualise a tomorrow
Better than, what it is today
With a lot to admire.

79. Ignite The Spark Within

The flame of knowledge, fuels a spark
To learning and finding a path
To get the wisdom, from the archives
Is to explore and find

To kindle the fire,
It seeks a burning desire
That comes from within
The expectations, of a bigger future
To surge and work for it

The inner being, speaks for you
It has a firm mindset, that dominates
You capture the true essence, of what's in sight
And light up, to let it sparkle
And enjoy it's glow

The way to get, your hearts desire
Is to not remain in the dark
Ignite and let the flames rise

To warm up your intellect, to use it
To a sprightly future ahead.

80. Change

The pen is mightier, than the sword
As a drop of ink can ignite a person's soul
Attitude and perceptions, can make achieve a million goals
Fresh ideas and new concepts, create an interesting read
And in turn a relaxed mind ,becomes more at ease

It is your attitude in life
That make you, or break you
If you want to make a change, in the world around you
How you live, is how you choose to be
Our acts are driven by the mind, you see
The best way to rejuvenate, is to smile and be carefree

Our social values are deep rooted, through our upbringing
Honesty, truth and universal harmony inclusive
Social integration, religious tolerance, deepen our understanding
To the community at large
To making personal and social values that last

To understand and relate to the world
And be conscious of reality, that has come to pass
The good, the bad and the choices we make

Are there to inspire and be inspired;
To making a change

Your sense of moral values are your nurturing ground
Commitment and responsibility, merged as one
To care and protect, in harmony with nature
And be humble, respectful, sensitive
To every human, animal and creature

Spirituality and universal brotherhood, comes from within us
Caring concern for our fellow beings
Includes the belief and hope in us
That we can, be the change
And the change lies within us.

81. Rhythms That Define

Music is the essence of life
Just as reading books that motivate and connect the mind
Books, music and writing have a lifelong influence

Music creates a rhythm
And the lyrics create a story
With both combined it
tugs at my heartstrings

Like writing is a passion
And life blends with music
And creates a lifelong sensation

With our fast paced life,
The art of reading is lost
As electronic gadgets, help us day in and day out
And being expressive is hidden
As every matter can be got, at the click of a button

Study shows that listening to music is a natural way of reducing
levels of stress
And the adrenaline released

Helps reduce the blood pressure
With increasing good anti bodies there after

Books and music, keep us engaged
As a friend to us, in trying times
They say patience is a virtue and listening is an art
Reading and lyrics convey better
So listen and make note,
As it enriches the heart

Reading books, has an influence
Just as writing, brings out expression
Music relaxes the body and mind
And all three combined ,mirrors your self image
While your mind, encourages you to be positive
And teaches you, valuable lessons in time

So hear and feel the beat of music
Like when in silence you read
The melody, the rhythm, the voices that reach
The echo, the speaker, the voracious reader
Reaching out is the writer, novelist, the singer and the song
Convey a message all along

The opera, the choir, the live band that entertains
The song writer, the author, who expresses from within

The adventures, the murder mysteries, a thriller or maybe a
bestseller to claim
An anthology, a poem, a rhyme or jingles to fame

Music, books go hand in hand
While they befriend you, when in gloom
An editor, a playwright, a poet, a composer
Always directs to get the reader and audience in rapt wonder
As each is out there to teach
To the stage and arena or just a library to reach

The paperbacks, the novels, the instruments, the voice
There's never a dearth for choice
For they keep you happy and pleased
As the price you pay for it,
Will always keep you away from boredom and at ease
For the wisdom gained is there to define,
Your interest in books and music
That drives the rhythm, of your life.

82. Vision of Life

Life that's diverse in many ways
Choose and rehearse, putting your best foot forward
When situations arise,
We need to Visualise
What's best to you, may not be for another
For the pathway could have hurdles and to some of us a burden

Not every move is a good one,
For life's battles to strive on
But make the most of it
It's hard but "work on"
As getting to enjoy life
The need is to survive
With dangers and tensions lurking by;
That suddenly come and make you stall
Putting everything that's planned, to a halt
It's only one life to lead
So make the better of it

There are times you wonder,
What the future holds
But take care anyway and never lose hope

As Rome was not built in a day
Face the world boldly but diligently
For the focus, is on the present
You learn from its past

It's human to make mistakes
And to correct the wrong to the right
Take baby steps to progress
To climb the ladder of success
So aim high and set the goal
To reach the target will take many a try
Do it anyways, one day at a time
And never let your enthusiasm die

Know your self worth and work at your skills
Focus in moving, if failure strikes
Never brood on your past, for its gone by
The future is your platform of what's yet to be
View the world presently
With the goal to achieve fully
Although the path ahead may seem rough
Fight to rain steadfast

Lead by example and set sail
Learn from your mistakes
As the journey of life has its ups and downs
Sometimes you achieve at times you drown

But remain afloat and believe in the best
Keep worries afar as at times your put to the test
Your vision to see
As life is often a mystery
So never give up, but accept gracefully

There isn't someone who is perfect
Many a time our hope deflates
So shirk the ego
And let go your pride
Reflect on your vision
And swim the tide
Create an attitude of positivity
Being indifferent to negativity
Grounded to reality
Grab all opportunities
For you never know when you get lucky
And pretty soon you will see
The best Vision of your life.

83. Evolve From the Ordinary

Beauty lies in the eyes of the beholder
Identity brings out a persona
It comes from within and with it I feel bolder
Charmed with a mystical aura
What's the sweet irony behind it ?
Is a question that makes me ponder
Leaving me wired to the views of the other

There's a vast expanse of beauty around us
Beauty of nature, with its flora and fauna
Bare grounds, meadows, forest and fields
Each having it's natural splendour
Unspoilt, but the greed of man has brought plunder

A butterfly that comes out if it's cocoon
Flutters from flower to flower
You glance at its beauty
Whether it's black, yellow, dotted or striped
There is nobody who can compare
The look of one to the other

We all admire, the winged beauty of nature!

So what in question is beautiful ?
And why do we compare ?
Black, white, brown or blue
We are all human
To get it straight, we need to reason
We all have, the same flesh and blood
And distinct features
So let not anybody compare
Your looks by your skin and colour
Or get trapped by stereo type views
But admit that beauty is not skin deep
As it comes from within

We all are just people, at the end of day
Who get moulded with time
The world's a big stage
We are the actors and each a role to play
We cannot be labelled
Except from the good and bad
There are wide choices to make and mistakes do happen
From time to time;
So evolve from the ordinary
And take it in your stride
That every human is beautiful, from the inside.

84. Inner Voice

There is an inner voice calling
If we take heed and hear
Sometimes it's a strong message
At times it's a disguise
That echoes feelings, of what's in store

The mind is confused, by inner thoughts
Of what is right or what's going wrong
It's time to take control and remain strong
The dilemma, is what to choose
And be in the right frame of mind
To conquer your feelings and let loose

Keeping your fears aside,
Make a note of and hear the call
As at times luck favours the brave
So take a bold step, with caution
With a definite goal and target to aim

There are voices that disturb you
And you get boggled at heart
Shatter your dreams and break them apart

Making you wonder, what's best to seek
Waking you from your slumber
With not knowing what's yonder;

At times the voice will beck and call you
And scream to hold tight, to your convictions
Or sometimes meek voices that suffice
And waver adding more confusion
But go by your gut feeling and intuition
Of what's best to your hearing
Work hard at your passions,
For there's no turning back the clock
The inner voice, says it all.

85. Bound By Chains

Our thoughts are bound by, what others think
Society makes rules, that are linked and cannot be broken
So we have to adhere to listen, when spoken

Our mind is not free, to do our will
Breaking boundaries, is an ill
We are chained by social customs
Of what to dress and what to eat

Going against cultural norms,
Is a definite taboo
Convicted and dispelled,
If you over step traditions
That do not meet, society's needs and expectations

There is a strong patriarchy
That limits women
Wagging and gossiping tongues, that profess
Of what rules, to form and digress

Gender inequality of men as superior
That women, should remain home and no further

Whose to change, this narrow mentality
And break the chains of disparity

Although these rigid barriers, are broken
It does curtail, the freedom to express
Of what is customary of you
If you are born a female

So let's just get our thought processes, to reason
To empower women
And not put a stop, to education
Unlock and change perceptions;
Drive a sense, that all genders are one and inclusive

Encourage women, to pursue their passions
And persevere, their dreams and aspiration
For the hand that rocks the cradle
Rules the world.

86. My Mind My Canvas

My mind is my possession
Sometimes clear and sometimes seized by obsession
The inner recesses of thoughts are deep
And surface in the subconscious
To lie dormant, unless you take a peek

At times distressed and other times in focus
If only we could paint, a beautiful picture
With a world that is colourful by nature,
Taking life, as an adventure.
Which brings out your true character

To mirror your self image
As a window to your dreams
To seek, to find that inner being
Which depicts an abstract or still life
Or just an empty canvas that needs brush strokes to beautify

You are the painter, the artist that aids
The constant patience that can create
Bring out your emotions, feelings and drive

To present an object of awe and delight

Your exhibit comes and is sourced from within
From a pathway that could have obstacles or humps
But to ride over these, it may take many a bump
Your presence of mind is what you must rely on

Make every picture your best one
True to yourself, never letting anything to chance
Work with determination and make a good presentation
As creating a masterpiece is a talent
The mind does not rest until completion.

87. A Time To Treasure

Time does not wait, it's ticking away
Do what you have to do today
As time past cannot be got back
Make time in the present, while it's here to stay

Don't put off or procrastinate, what's important to do
Never wait for the future, as you cannot foresee its timing
For time well spent
Is a treasure to having

Time and tide, wait for no man
It runs fast, so does the tide
So keep everything, precisely timed
Make good use of it
As life teaches you in time
Time is the ticker;
Invest in time to make it better

Time once lost never returns
As it's the greatest gift of all
So spend quality time, be it work, family or in a relationship

Time heals everything, have the patience

There is a time to sow and a time to reap
Time it well, to perfection
Yesterday's time is gone and lost
And even harder, to retrieve
So make the best of today's time;
For time stops at nothing
If you are not inclined, to its timing

The past cannot be changed,
But the future is in your power
With proper planning of hours
So do not waste time brooding, on what is to come
Stop to rest if you must
But know that time wasted
Is a time forgotten that goes fast.

88. Turn of Generations

Life is like a pathway
We design the road
Everyday is not the same,
Varied by era and decades that age

We have seen a bullock cart
Taken a joy ride, as it slowly wound its way
Seen untarred roads and lanes
Cycled in terrains that led to nowhere

Uncut trees, that blossomed full bloom
Nature and greenery, untouched by urbanisation
During the generation of Baby boomers, before world War two
An era that focussed on ,just security
Conservative and cautious, with concerns of safety

Then came the Millennials the generation X
Where we saw rapid inventions
And aspirations ,with a desire to excel
After which came Gen Z
Post millennials with a zest

At present is generation Alpha
Awaiting trips to space and Mars
Rapid technology with improved science
And internet drives, with apps that are ample
Looking at it now, it all looks simple

To help derive information
Is at your hands reach
And gain access to knowledge
Communication, has got better
Gadgets that have made life easier

As we have seen generations go fast
Using smart technology
And remote controlled, robots and cars
Alexa and Siri, that answer in a jiffy
Wifi and bluetooth that help connect, the world at large
That is futuristic and smart.

89. The Power of Friendship

Some memories are still fresh
And are here to stay
Specially of the good times, you have had with friends
That bring back happiness and do not perish with time

Friendship and bonding, come from those who love you
This caring does not hurt you
Like family, that stays close at heart
Distance and time, does not break them apart

There are many friends, that you encounter in life
Some walk in and out sometime
Good friends are like precious gifts,
Hard to keep and even harder to find

But true friendship is priceless
And stays with you, when everyone deserts you
Reaching out, when you need help
So they become impossible to forget

Lifelong friendships ,go way back to love
Seasons and months sometimes years, without meeting
Never question this friendship;
Regardless of how far they live
A good friend remains a best friend, till the end

A simple pat, a handshake, a hug and embrace
Lifts up your spirits when lonely
A friend alone can understand,
When your hurt and sympathise
And give a listening ear, to empathise

Best friends are like family, never lose them
Share your feelings and emotions with them
They are sincere and never judge
Leave footprints and never grudge

Sometimes when broken and shaken up
Friends are there to communicate
So they are your treasure
As they pour out love ,without measure

Friends are your lifeline,
Some are sincere and true
So make friends whom you can trust,
That will keep friendships that last.

90. Cradle of Survival

The struggle of survival exists
Cradled by the mother, from the womb
With relative stability, through nine months of gestation time
The maternal instincts of mom, is no surprise
To nurture and sacrifice

It's inborn and instant
To love unconditionally
She endures patience and understanding
That come to her naturally
To protect and always remain steadfast, to mothering

Oxytocin and happiness hormone is released
Have an impact ,on bonding
Leading to feelings, of well being
A degree of change in the brain structure;
Creates an instinct in the mother

Your identity, on becoming a mom
Is derived from your strengths and character
To being compassionate and caring
Putting your child's need, before your own

To giving your best, is a skill to hone

Attachment comes, over a period of time
With strong emotional ties being made secure
A relationship that bind,s will always remain constant
With every passing year

The infant, the child, the teen , the youth and adult
At every stage, needs a guide
It's mother they turn to, for support and advice
So the role of a mother played, is an important one
In the upbringing of her offspring
And her future progeny, will be a happy one.

91. Circle of Hope

When I throw up my hands in despair
My mind is in turmoil, of what's next
The roots of faith run deep
Losing hope will make you, crawl and creep

With years of toil, you don't want to give up
As you've put in hard work, from the sweat of your brow
So take courage and put your head to thought
That giving up is not the best solution
To getting results

A learning curve is an experience
With hurdles in between
If you are passionate with conviction
And grounded to commitment
You come out victorious at the end

The labour of love, takes time to blossom
Faith and hope is the key
Like a plant that needs to be nurtured;
Which takes time to grow

The ultimate success to show

Many a lesson is learnt
If you go beyond your comfort zone
There are many ways, to conquer
And let go off your qualms
Seek to find an answer
To give new hope to your dreams

So let your wishes, be discovered
And faith be stronger
As life is like a roller coaster
It circles by twists and turns
But at the end, it brings out the best
And a sense of thrill and achievement
That circles your hope of fulfilment.

92. Path To Recovery

The path to recovery is lonesome,
While you are shattered and broken
You need to fix the pieces, that are scattered
And gather them one by one
Lifting up your spirits and remain strong

Sometimes your health, could go for a toss
While you are at a loss
It takes time to recover
And get a complete makeover
To get back to normal
In your fight for survival

At times the path becomes a long road, that seems endless
Don't give up nevertheless
Staying calm you get over your anxiety
To remain in control of yourself
Should become your priority

Mental health and wellbeing go hand in hand
Beat the stress and the pain
Most of us go through these ups and downs

Of anger, moods and depression
You are not the only one in this situation

Share your feelings and get connected
Seek help from a professional or friend
There is no shame in sharing your emotions
Get answers by expressing your concerns

The mind is confused by the choices we have made
At times you succeed, other times you fail
It is not unusual to face struggles
Handle them well from getting out of hand
Take the path of recovery and see happiness at the end.

93. Pursuit of Art

An artists perception is a creation
Be it on paper, sculpture, ceramic it's a representation
Throwing light and depicting
Ones innate feeling, while expressing

The world is it's palette
That gives a picture to define
The colours painted are glimpses ,of a varied kind
That underlay one's character and mind

Art is in different forms
The richness of the canvas
Lies in the hands of the painter,
Creating a vast definition of culture

Some are objects, that have still life
A landscape that's beautiful
Or a seascape, which leaves you mesmerised
Maybe an abstract, that's surreal
That keeps you engrossed by the form it takes;

The Potter turns the moulded clay

The wheel that moves round, has a firm grip
By hands and legs that use skill
To turn it into a sculpture for display

The keen eye that grasps,
Creates and throws light on the past
By having a impact, on the present
From the beauty of it's exhibits

Each stroke of the brush
Completed and visualises a frame
In working to get, the artistic touch
While the mind connects to the brain.

94. Voice That Echoes

The voice vents out emotions
At times cries for help
There are limitations, to its waking
While it voices out opinions
At times it is solitary, sometimes it represents a community

The voices of the marginalised
Remain always silenced
The underprivileged are at a loss for words
The echoes of their voices, are never heard
Labour class and the migrants face a crisis
Their sentiments hurt, in tough circumstances

There's the gentle voice, that gives a reminder
That all humans need to be heard
Or a screaming voice, that needs an answer
When everything fails to respond,
To social issues that matter
Address and express feelings;
Is the stronger voice, that comes from within

There are voices left weakened

When curtailed or stopped from speaking
These voices hesitate
And remain discreet, when calling
Or not communicate, when disturbed
To get to be voiceless and perturbed

The voice that's heard
Is the voice that challenges head on
Will reach far out and is feared
It will instigate, and move to direct
To get an identity of its own
While it resonates, to find a solution, to many a problem

So don't hesitate to speak and find
That every action, has a profound reaction
The voice that does not waver,
Will not dither or quiver
So speak out loud and clear
And make yourself, a voice, that echoes and be heard.

95. Precious Lessons

Of tsunamis and earthquakes,
That ravage the earth
And catastrophic destruction,
That cause displacement
By giant waves that engulf
With nature's fury berserk-
But the lessons we learnt from Covid 19
Is something that brought the world, to a standstill

The first wave saw deaths on the rise
To social distance oneself looked wise
The fear of what will be gripped by, the universe
And hands tied behind our backs, unable to decipher
The tiny virus spread out, its ugly tentacles
When people suffered around us
To get fragments, of their life together

These trying times there was anguish and despair
Where families huddled together to care
Lockdowns and restricted movements were brought in place
While we learnt to appreciate health

And social distance ourselves

Work from home became a common scene
Life was hanging in various strands of confused thoughts
With the change in lifestyle to remain cautious
Covered to mask and be diligent
When the media blared out news of people succumbing
And hospital beds got filled to recouping

To adhere to these norms brought discipline
To be rigid in our movements to caution
When funeral pyres were lit and morgues were filled to the brim
The spirits of gloom became palpable
As these lessons taught that lives were valuable

Medical theories and science technologies were brought to the
forefront
Vaccines became the order of the day
An attempt to change our carefree ways
The world learnt how to manage a pandemic
Although with doubts of its implications
These deep dark moments brought the world to shambles
Also awakened our senses

And everyone went online
With many a talent nurtured in time
From schooling to teaching to meetings and schedules

Everything was handled on various apps and zoom
And to sanitise and wash hands
To keep the virus at bay
Changed our perspective to life
And many precious lessons learnt
Stemmed from these dark experiences.

96. Look Beyond

Look beyond, there is a rise in temperature
Fossil fuel burning brings about excessive danger
Release of toxic fumes, cloud the atmosphere
Rapidly melting the ice glaciers

With weather patterns changing
It gives the earth, a clear warning
As it's harmful to humans, animals and nature
Carbon dioxide emissions, pollute the air
As global warming, raises its ugly head

Deforestation, leads to soil erosion
Loss of plants and other vegetation
Increase in floods, due to heavy rainfall
Causing severe drought, due to failure of crops
And intensity of storms, destroy our existence

It's a matter of grave concern
As this threat to human life, cannot be justified
It's created by greenhouse gases,
That bring a change in weather patterns
Rising heat waves and sea levels

Cause extreme flooding and Tsunami, that cause havoc

The future of the earth, is at stake
Don't postpone until it quakes
The greenhouse effect ,blocks the sun's rays
Bringing extreme heat and intense cold
That are a threat to atmosphere

So plant more trees and save the earth
Do not ignore it's cry or calling
The magnitude of its destruction,
Is spoiling the environment
So take heed and make amends, at saving our planet.

97. What's Your Medicine

For a good healthy body
You need to have the drive
Come what may, it's life's desire
To look young and strive
Maintain a balance of wellness
To burn up the fat inside

Your weight in question?
A tummy tuck
An hourglass figure
A slim figure, a model look
Is only for those, who exercise
And get cravings under control

A little indulgence, isn't bad
Chocolate sometimes to have
Total sugar rush isn't good
Sitting on the couch,
With no exercise at all

Makes you obese and your health to deteriorate

Eat healthy check your scale,
Maintain a strict regime
Cut down on carbs,
Strengthen your abs
It's the rigmarole, of setting a routine
To get your body metabolism straight

The bitter pill, the aerobic drill
The gym equipments ,that keep you walking the treadmill
Ensures you get, to being healthy and fit
The yoga teachers that recommend
Of stretching poses, to make your body bend

What's your gut feeling ?
While your rejuvenating
To have immunity is a challenge
As your gut health has a direct impact;
In absorbing vital nutrients,
That add fuel to your digestion

There's a whole lot of supplements
Available, over the pharmacy counter
From probiotics, to protein shakes
That enhance and boost your vitality
Good bacteria, that can fight, your resistance to illness

And meet your goals, of reducing faster

Vitamins and essential medicines supply lot of nutrients
Act as defence mechanisms,
To your daily diet regimen
Food that's nutritious and organic
Are a rich source of probiotic
That improve your physical health overall

But what's more significant
Is your mental health and well being
That stems and takes root, from within
Laughter they say, is the best medicine
That keeps you happy and content

So keep self control, on your food intake
Your mind relaxed and free from stress
Enjoy nature's walks in the sun, with gratitude
Take adequate sleep and rest;
As it's your gateway to robust health.

98. Anchor To Survival

The year 2020 saw many a life lost
When corona struck, it's deadly claws
The world was put to silence
With curfews in place
And people feared the ultimate
Knowing, that the virus claimed
And lives were at stake
To rising deaths, destiny and fate

Migrant workers took exodus
As lockdowns were enforced
They travelled long distances on foot,
To finding their homes
They felt displaced by gloom,
As the sudden surge, in positive cases
Predicted would take a toll

Health care workers and doctors struggled
And stayed put in hospitals
Equipped with disposable masks and bodysuits;
Fighting hard to save lives
With many dying before their eyes,

Ambulances with sirens beeped
With many lives lost, in a sweep

Sale of oximeters and booking of ICU beds
Brought people to monitor, their breathing
To be hospitalised with fear gripped
This wake up call for vaccines,
Raised alarm bells to distress;
With question mark, of it's side effects

The world by then felt shaken up
And pharma companies vied to sell
To vaccination as the new norm
As to gather in groups, was out of bounds

Marriages turned to be small affair
With just close family and friends
The glamour and glitz, of extravagance was lost
With corona warnings, to distance
Although many of us ,felt the grip of it's impact
We went back to the grind
And countries, opened up to visitors
With airports that had shut down ,brought flights back on

As the year passed quickly
While we remained strictly,
Without knowing, what was to be

To avoid crowds and follow covid appropriate behaviour
We anchored ourselves, to caution and wait
To survive the yea,r that went by in a haste.

99. The Big Picture

The big picture ain't always good
There's failure and doubt
Awards and accolades are there,
For many in this world to stare
But the big picture is not complete
If you have not felt it's worth within

Your life is your testament,
Even when you stumble and fall
Sometimes you step, on turbulent waters
And struggle on and off
So battle your problems wisely
And focus to make amends,
To start over again

Life's journey isn't rosy
It has its faults
Keep working hard, at your goals
Take a grip on your thoughts
You may not see, the result as yet
As the picture does not look pretty

Without a frame in place

So patience is the key
With many a triumph
Hold on to its victories;
As the picture you portray
Brings happiness in time
As it falls in place, with determination and grit sometime

A picture brings out emotions,
If you don't pursue
Be aware of its flaws,
That curtail and bring you down
Make you reason and frown
Pose with conviction and do not feel disdain
For its like the mirror, that reflects
So know that nobody is perfect
So portray a good picture instead.

100. My Past My Future

My past lies before me
Like an open book to see
But only, I remember, what was in its pages
And see the history, it left as a memory
The past nurtured me, to what I am today
The future is unknown to me

The past taught many lessons
Made me bold by experiences
Some talents that I had got wasted
But not regret and fret, was what I learnt
As there's always room, for opportunity
That needs to be tried and tested
As you never know what lies ahead
Could keep you at your best

Not every childhood is a happy one
But a child grows and never complains
For your grown to be, what you are today
Never give room for bad memories, keep them far away
Don't be imprisoned ,by your bad thoughts

As it can lead you astray

A traumatic past, you may encounter
May have left you prisoned and conquered
By unwanted fears, of it's outcome
But tapping your passions
Keeps you focused and can be therapy
Against fighting your emotions,
That left a void in your present

Sure you know, what you are good at
Try and test new waters and explore
Give vent to your feelings
Sometimes even, let out a cry
The choices you make, will define you as a person
And keep your mind stronger, in unison

The present throws light to your future
May look bleak, with new variants lurking
From Corona, to Delta, to Omicron
And probably more in the offing
They are named, like the different storms
That strike each time to destroy
But as luck favours the brave, we need to take precautions to
save

So keep your immunity in check

Savour the time that comes, going with the flow
The past lies dormant, like an unopened box
To view when chanced upon;
If only we could heed to its present call
And find a way that leads, to a future overall.

www.ingramcontent.com/pod-product-compliance
Lightning Source LLC
Chambersburg PA
CBHW020913160726
47993CB00005B/1946